COPING™

I0811996

COPING WITH

TICK-BORNE DISEASES

Marcia Amidon Lusted

Rosen YA™
New York

Published in 2020 by The Rosen Publishing Group, Inc.
29 East 21st Street, New York, NY 10010

First Edition

Library of Congress Cataloging-in-Publication Data

Names: Lusted, Marcia Amidon, author.
Title: Coping with tick-borne diseases / Marcia Amidon Lusted.
Description: New York : Rosen Publishing, 2020. | Series: Coping | Audience: Grades 7–12. | Includes bibliographical references and index.
Identifiers: LCCN 2018049633 | ISBN 9781508187370 (library bound) | ISBN 9781508187363 (pbk.)
Subjects: LCSH: Tick-borne diseases—Juvenile literature.
Classification: LCC RA641.T5 L87 2020 | DDC 614.4/33—dc23
LC record available at https://lccn.loc.gov/2018049633

Manufactured in the United States of America

CONTENTS

INTRODUCTION

Most people are used to dealing with pests like mosquitoes and blackflies. These pests might cause an irritating bite or two. They are mostly an itchy annoyance. But there is another outdoor pest that is steadily increasing in number. This pest can cause much more serious illnesses for animals and people who are bitten by it. It's ticks! And no matter where someone lives in the United States, or even the world, there is at least one species of tick that can cause serious illness or even death.

Most Americans did not pay a great deal of attention to tick-borne illnesses until the discovery of Lyme disease in the 1970s. Even then, most people did not take any particular precautions when they played or worked outside. Lyme disease was difficult to diagnose and its symptoms were vague. This meant that those who did contract the disease often had difficulty getting medical help. Their symptoms would last for years, sometimes causing further damage.

Louis was only eight years old when he was bitten by a tick in 2007, after he and his family got a new puppy. He told his story on the Bay Area Lyme Foundation website:

Ticks, like this adult deer tick, were once just another annoying insect. But now scientists know that they transmit diseases, and they are becoming an increasing problem all over the country.

We didn't know much about the woods and the ticks in them. I would roll in the leaves while playing with my puppy. She was a tick magnet. It wasn't long before I had a tick on me … In February, I started having real trouble with exhaustion and joint pain. At one point I could not walk and had to crawl.

Deer are one of the biggest tick carriers. Due to an increasing number of housing developments and a decrease in wilderness areas, deer are coming into more contact with humans.

I had dizziness too and trouble thinking in class. My mom took me to the pediatrician. He insisted it wasn't Lyme disease … [Louis's mom finally found a doctor who tested him for Lyme disease, and he was treated for a year and a half before feeling normal again.] My mom says she remembers the day my personality came back. I had been so sick that I disappeared for a while.

Ticks are increasing in number around the world. And humans are at increasing risk of contracting serious diseases from ticks. This means it is more important than ever for people to be aware of

A hike in the woods with friends now includes the risk of being bitten by ticks and becoming ill. Take precautions, such as using insect repellent and wearing proper clothing, before hiking.

ticks. It is also important to learn to protect oneself outside and to learn what to do if one is bitten by a tick. Checking yourself and your animals for ticks after being outside must become a regular part of everyone's routine. The days of going outside to play in the backyard or hike in the woods without insect repellent or proper clothing are over. But that doesn't mean that enjoying the outdoors is no longer possible. With knowledge and prevention, tick-borne illnesses in both people and animals can be avoided. With a little preparation, all can still enjoy the natural world around them.

CHAPTER ONE

One Summer in Connecticut

The summer of 1975 was a typical one in Connecticut. Warm, sunny days. Kids swimming, exploring the woods, and playing outside in backyards and fields. Adults were also enjoying the outdoors. They hiked in the woods and played with their children.

However, for people who lived in Lyme, Connecticut, or the surrounding areas of Old Lyme and East Haddam, the summer of 1975 would be different. According to the article "History of Lyme Disease," by the Bay Area Lyme Foundation, that summer would have a lasting effect on them—and on the world. That fall, a group of twelve adults and thirty-nine children from this area began to suffer from some unusual symptoms.

Old Lyme, Connecticut, was one of the first places where Lyme disease appeared in 1975. Today Lyme disease is a major health problem all over the United States and in other parts of the world.

These symptoms couldn't be easily traced to a specific cause. They included skin rashes, headaches, and severe fatigue. More puzzling symptoms, such as swollen knees and paralysis, also occurred. Doctors suspected that perhaps the thirty-nine children included in this group were suffering from some form of juvenile rheumatoid arthritis. But that was not a disease that tended to occur in clusters in a particular location. No one knew exactly what was causing the symptoms or how to treat them.

Searching for Answers

The orthopedic doctor in the area had no idea what he was seeing. "He had a different answer for everyone," Todd Murray, who was one of the afflicted children, told Jarret Liotta from *National Geographic* magazine. Todd's mother, Polly Murray, along with one other extremely concerned mother from the area, finally contacted the state's health department.

In August 1976, the Connecticut State Department of Health became concerned about the strange illness. It issued a letter to the state's directors of health. It characterized the geographical distribution of the illness:

> *There were 4.3 cases per 1,000 residents in Old Lyme, Lyme and East Haddam. Cases tended to occur among persons living near heavily wooded and sparsely settled areas, not in the town centers or on Long Island Sound. On some roads as many as 10 children were affected. Most of those affected had the onset of their symptoms in the summer or early fall.*

The letter went on to speculate that the geographic distribution, and the seasonal occurrence of the symptoms, suggested that it might have been caused by a virus that was carried by biting insects. It stated that the department of health and Yale scientists were now studying the cases. The scientists were trying to identify the virus. And because these were appropriate actions, any other action "would disrupt the community far more than is warranted by facts." In other words, they did not want any more publicity for the illness. They did not want to upset people in the area, even though it might be very important that people avoid certain areas.

Lyme Arthritis

Polly Murray contacted Yale because she wanted to help her son. Because of her outreach, and because of the department of health's investigation, a Yale scientist named Allen Steere began to study the symptoms. Dr. Steere called the mysterious illness Lyme arthritis. He chose this name because of the arthritis-like symptoms of pain and swelling in the joints.

According to Shana Elbaum-Garfinkle in the article "Close to Home: A History of Yale and Lyme Disease," published in the *Yale Journal of Biology and*

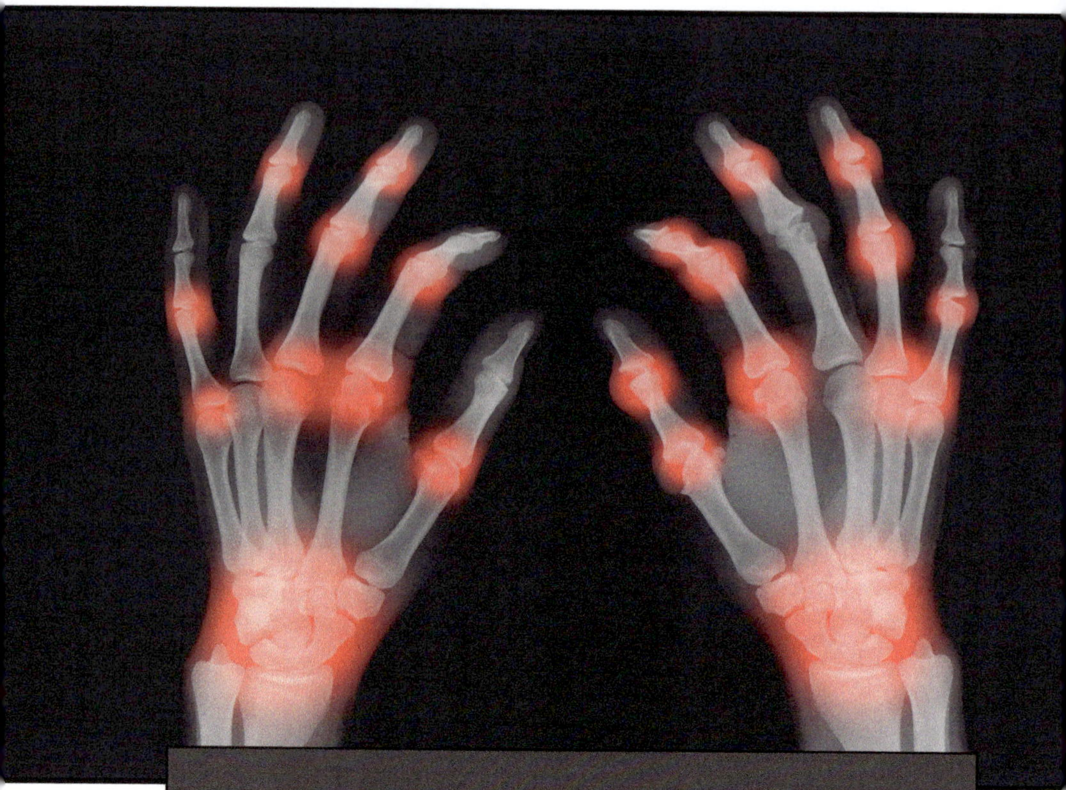

Lyme disease was first called Lyme arthritis because it caused pain and swelling in joints, similar to arthritis. This scan shows areas where hand and finger joints have swollen.

Medicine, Steere and his Yale colleague Dr. Stephen E. Malawista began investigating the outbreak of the mysterious symptoms. Both doctors worked in Yale's Department of Rheumatology. Rheumatology is the study of disorders of joints, muscles, and ligaments and illnesses such as arthritis. They conducted physical examinations and laboratory tests on the forty-nine people from Lyme, Old Lyme, and East Haddam. They also did personal interviews. Though the lab work did not reveal anything notable, the personal interviews did. The doctors learned that almost a quarter of the patients reported having a bull's-eye-shaped ring of rash on their skin weeks before the first arthritis symptoms occurred. Most of the patients lived in wooded areas of their towns. This was the clue that the doctors needed to make a connection.

The unusual bull's-eye rash was a characteristic of tick bites that had been studied in Europe. Those bites produced symptoms like nerve pain and paralysis. However, in Europe these tick bites had never been associated with arthritis symptoms. Steere and Malawista believed they had encountered a new type of tick-borne disease. And it was a vector-borne disease. This meant that it was transmitted by the bite of an infected insect, such as mosquitoes, ticks, triatomine bugs, sandflies, and blackflies. Excited by their findings, the two Yale doctors waited for the next season when ticks and other insects would once again be active. And in the summer of

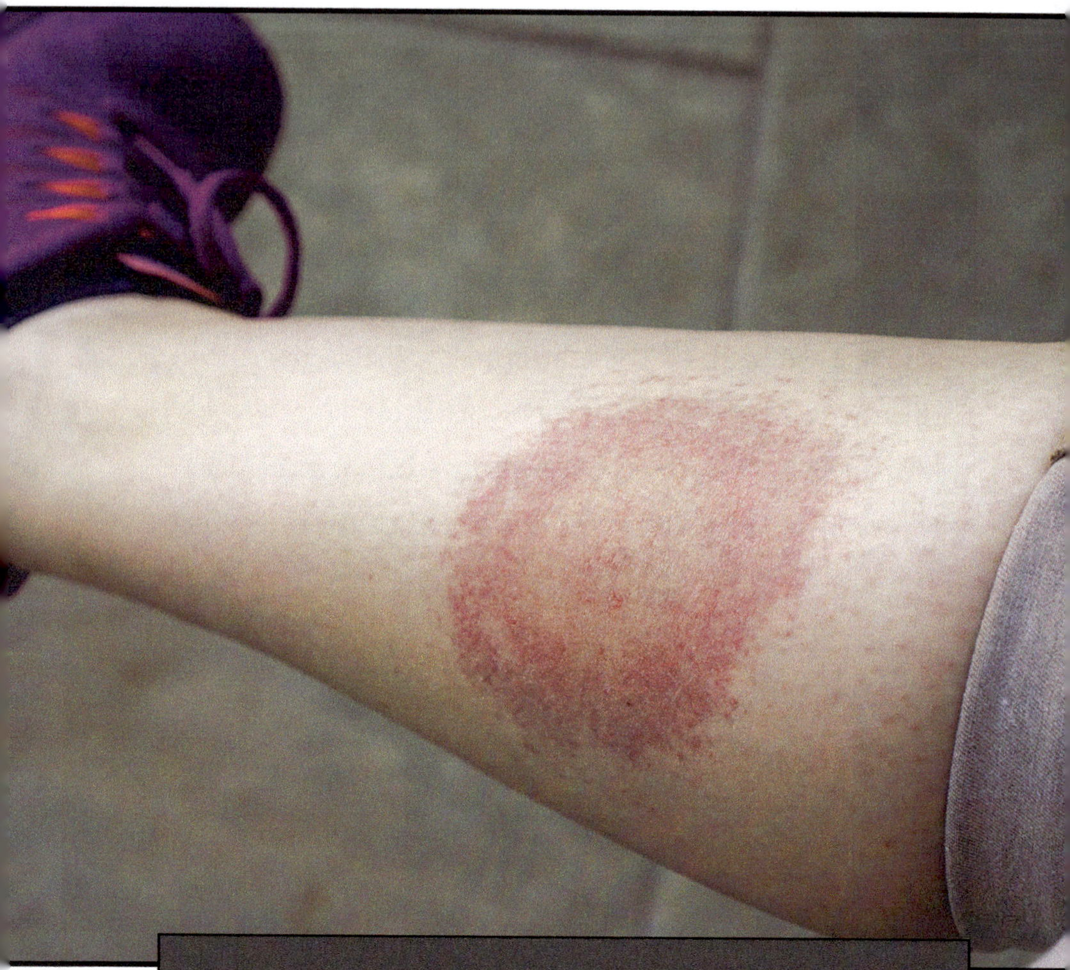

Tick-borne diseases like Lyme disease create a distinctive bull's-eye rash on the skin at the site of the tick bite. The rash is an important symptom that requires a visit to the doctor.

1976, there were thirty new patients from the same geographical area. Steere and Malawista now felt there was a definite connection between the bite of a tick and the arthritis-like symptoms. They began calling the disease Lyme arthritis.

A Tick Conspiracy Theory

There is a controversial theory about why ticks carrying Lyme disease suddenly appeared in Connecticut in 1975, which Jarret Liotta wrote about in *National Geographic.* About 8 miles (13 kilometers) south of Lyme, Connecticut, is the Plum Island Animal Disease Center. It was originally operated by the US Army, then by the Department of Agriculture, and now by the Department of Homeland Security. The center does research related to agricultural bioterrorism. Some people believe that it was experimenting with using ticks to carry diseases and act as biological agents for germ warfare. They blame the sudden occurrence of Lyme disease on the accidental release of these infected ticks.

Tracking Ticks

Once the Yale team discovered that Lyme arthritis was being transmitted by ticks, the resarchers were able to link it to the deer tick. They studied the area in

Connecticut where the first symptoms had appeared. They could tell that there were more incidents of Lyme arthritis in areas with a higher population of deer and deer ticks. The deer tick, known by its scientific name *Ixodes scapularis,* is only the size of a poppy seed. The deer tick carries a bacterium from a group of bacteria called spirochetes.

At the time, a scientist named William Burgdorfer was studying Rocky Mountain spotted fever, which is also caused by a tick bite. In 1982, he isolated the spirochete that caused the Lyme symptoms: *Borrelia burgdorferi.* The sudden increase in ticks and the symptoms of Lyme arthritis could be linked to an

Celebrity Sufferers

Many celebrities have suffered from Lyme disease and have gone public in order to raise awareness of the illness. They want people to know how common it is. According to Winona

Dimeo-Ediger's 2017 article in *Rolling Stone,* Kelly Osbourne, Alec Baldwin, Avril Lavigne, Kathleen Hanna, Yolanda Hadid (along with her daughter Bella and son Anwar), Kris Kristofferson, Ben Stiller, Shania Twain, and Debbie Gibson are among those who have publicized their illnesses. They hope to emphasize the need for prevention and diagnosis.

Yolanda Hadid (*left*) and Bella Hadid (*right*), both Lyme disease sufferers, attend the United for a Lyme-Free World event in New York City in 2016. The event raises awareness of tick-borne illnesses.

increase in the population of deer. This is because the ticks had to feed on deer in order to reproduce.

Doctors in the Connecticut area were now told to report any similar symptoms to the Yale doctors. As they began studying these patients, they realized that arthritis was just one of the symptoms of this new disease. In addition to affecting the joints, it could also affect the nervous system and the heart. So the new disease was renamed Lyme disease. In 1984, Yale held the first international conference on Lyme disease. Experts in rheumatology, immunology, dermatology, and neurology, as well as public health officials and practicing physicians, attended.

Lyme Disease Today

Scientists continue to study Lyme disease. Lyme disease can be classified as either early or late, according to how long the patient has had it. Early Lyme disease starts with the initial circular rash, and then in a few days or weeks it includes symptoms like headaches, fatigue, and fever. Late Lyme disease is when the disease progresses to arthritis symptoms and the swelling of the joints. Later Lyme disease can also include more serious symptoms, such as cardiac problems. If the disease is caught early, such as with the discovery of the bull's-eye rash, it can be successfully treated with antibiotics most of the time. But not every patient gets a rash or notices it. This makes it more difficult to diagnose the disease at later stages, when antibiotics may not be as effective.

Since the 1980s, reports of Lyme disease have been increasing dramatically. Lyme disease is now one of the biggest public health concerns in the United States. According to the Centers for Disease Control and Prevention (CDC), it is estimated that there are 106 cases of Lyme disease per 100,000 people every year. This makes for a total of about 329,000 new cases annually. The highest rates of the disease are among boys ages five to nine and people of both sexes who are between sixty and sixty-four. Many towns and cities are trying to control the deer population as a way to reduce the tick population. But in many parts of the country, Lyme disease is an increasingly large risk for anyone who spends time outdoors. People who have pets like dogs, which

Scientists are studying the rise in tick-borne illnesses to better understand how they are transmitted. They are seeking more effective treatment and possible vaccines.

might bring ticks indoors on their fur, are also at risk. And what was once an East Coast disease has now been found around the country and even in Hawaii.

Scientists are still studying Lyme disease. Some scientists feel the increase in incidence of the disease is connected to climate change. There is also the appearance of new strains of the bacteria and new tick species that are transmitting Lyme-like illnesses. Laboratory tests are not reliable when it comes to recognizing the bacteria. Symptoms can be very different from patient to patient, and treatments like long-term antibiotic use can actually harm a patient's health over time. All of this needs to be studied more.

According to Dr. Rebecca Eisen, a research biologist, in an article "Lyme and other tickborne diseases," issued by the CDC:

> *Since the late 1990s, the number of reported cases of Lyme disease in the United States has tripled and the number of counties in the northeastern and upper Midwestern United States that are considered high-risk for Lyme disease has increased by more than 300%. One explanation for this trend is that the ticks that can transmit Lyme disease have expanded their geographic range and are now being found in places they weren't seen 20 years ago. This makes it more important than ever for people to take steps to prevent tick bites, particularly during the spring and summer when ticks are most active.*

More than Just Lyme

Lyme disease receives a great deal of attention because it is a relatively new disease. It is also becoming very common. But it is not the only tick-borne disease that is on the increase in the United States. Lyme disease is found mostly in the Northeast, mid-Atlantic, and upper Midwest states, but the range where these ticks are being found is increasing. Other tick-borne illnesses commonly found in the United States include the following:

- Anaplasmosis is spread to humans by the black-legged tick. Anaplasmosis is mostly found in the upper Midwest and on the Pacific coast.
- Babesiosis is caused by the same black-legged ticks and results in microscopic parasites that infect red blood cells. This disease is mostly found in the Northeast and upper Midwest.
- Ehrlichiosis is transmitted by the lone star tick, found in south central and eastern US states.
- Powassan virus is passed to humans in the Northeast and Great Lakes area by the black-legged tick and the groundhog tick.
- Rocky Mountain spotted fever is transmitted by the American dog tick, the Rocky Mountain wood tick, and the brown dog tick.
- Tick-borne relapsing fever (TBRF) is transmitted through the bites of infected soft ticks and has been reported in fifteen states. It is usually associated with sleeping in rough, rustic cabins or vacation homes.

There are many more tick-borne illnesses found in the United States as well.

Ticks by the Numbers

- In total, the CDC received reports of 642,602 cases of sixteen different tick-borne diseases in the United States from 2004 to 2016.
- Nine of these diseases were being reported for the first time in the United States. The CDC stressed that the diseases are most likely underreported because people aren't always aware of tick bites or the symptoms that can result.
- Tick-borne diseases have more than doubled in thirteen years.
- Tick-borne diseases also account for 77 percent of all the vector-caused illnesses (which include diseases transmitted by mosquitoes).

Additionally, tick-borne diseases are difficult to control or treat, and there are no vaccines associated with tick-borne diseases. Ticks and mosquitoes are also becoming resistant to insecticides used to eliminate them.

Coming Soon to a Household Near You?

What does all this mean? It means that if you live in any part of the United States and spend any time outdoors, the chances are increasing that at some point you might be bitten by a tick. And that tick might possibly infect you with a tick-borne illness. So how do people cope with the possibility of tick infections? How does one deal with the reality of a tick-borne illness once he or she has contracted it? Prevention and treatment begin with understanding just how something as tiny as a tick can transmit something as potentially life changing or even life altering as one of these diseases.

CHAPTER TWO

The Trouble with Ticks

It's easy to think that tick-borne illnesses are a new threat to humans. After all, many adults can remember a time when ticks weren't a big problem. But researchers have found writing about tick-borne illnesses from as early as 1550 BCE. Ancient Egyptian papyrus scrolls talk about "tick fever." Ancient Greeks like Cato, Aristotle, and Pliny referred to ticks as "disgusting parasites." The ability of ticks to carry diseases to humans has been recognized for hundreds of years. But it wasn't until 1893 that two researchers, Theobald Smith and Frederick L. Kilbourne, conducted experiments that scientifically linked Texas cattle fever to a specific tick, *Boophilus annulatus*. This major scientific study proved that parasitic arthropods could carry and transmit infectious organisms just through feeding on the blood of a host animal.

Lyme disease was officially discovered in 1975. But researchers from Yale University discovered that the Lyme disease bacterium has actually been circulating through New England forests for sixty thousand years. That is long before humans arrived! The bacterium once moved among animal hosts in the forests. It began to reach people when they moved into rural areas during the twentieth century. The increase in the deer population, partly due to the loss of predators like wolves and hunting restrictions, also increased the tick population. Finally, the changing and warming climate has accelerated the tick's growth cycles. It has also allowed them to move farther and farther north.

The World of Arthropods

Just what is an arthropod? An arthropod is a class of animals, including insects, crustaceans, and arachnids, that make up 75 percent of the life on our planet. They are the most successful animals to inhabit Earth. They live on land, sea, and air. There

Amber, the hardened sap of trees, can contain fossilized remains of arthropods that are millions of years old. Researchers have studied ticks caught in amber to see if they carried illnesses, too.

are more than one million species of arthropods, including spiders, insects, centipedes, mites, lobsters, crabs, shrimp, crayfish, krill, barnacles, scorpions … and ticks.

Arthropods have segmented bodies in two or three sections. They also have an exoskeleton, which is an external skeleton that protects the soft insides of their bodies, much like armor. This makes them invertebrates because they do not have an inside backbone, as humans do. Arthropods are born with soft shells that quickly harden and can be shed as they grow bigger. They have many jointed legs or limbs, and they are cold-blooded. There are eleven different scientific classes of arthropods. Ticks belong to the class Arachnida, along with spiders and mites.

The Three Tick Families

- Ticks themselves can be categorized into three families. Each family has different behaviors. Ixodidae, or "hard ticks," have a hard body covering. Ixodids attach themselves to a host and remain there, feeding, for several days. Their bite does not hurt, and they may not be easily noticed. They usually live from several months to three years.
- Argasidae, or "soft ticks," have a flexible body covering. Argasids feed often, for shorter amounts of time, and usually on a single host species. They tend to live in dry areas, in sheltered sites near their hosts. They can survive for as long as ten years and are resistant to times of starvation.
- Nuttalliellidae so far exist as only a single species of tick found in Africa.

Life Stages

As arthropods, hard-bodied ticks go through four life stages:

1. Egg
2. Six-legged larva

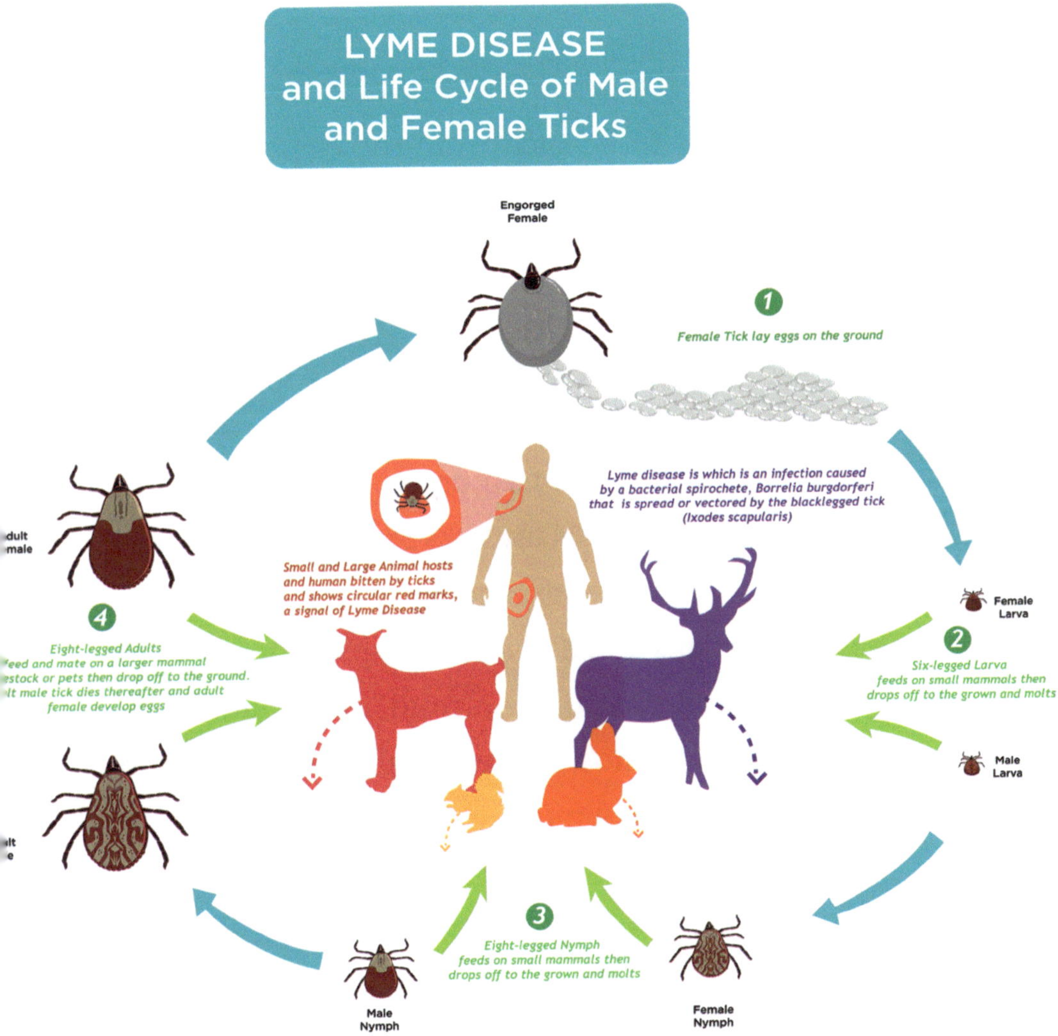

The above graphic shows the life cycle of ticks, their most common hosts, and when hosts are most likely to be infected. Ticks are more likely to attach themselves to hosts at certain points in their life cycles.

3. Eight-legged nymph
4. Adult

As soon as they hatch from the egg, ticks must feed on the blood of a host at every stage of their lives to survive. Because they need so many hosts for the different stages of their lives, it can take three years for a tick to move through its life cycle. Many will die simply because they can't find a host when they require one. Ticks feed on reptiles, amphibians, mammals, and birds. Many ticks prefer different types of hosts at different stages in their life cycles.

How do ticks find the hosts on which they need to feed? They can detect the warmth, breath, and body odors of potential hosts. They can also sense vibration as the host animals move and even moisture from their bodies. Ticks can wait beside a well-used path for a potential host to come by. They can't leap or fly. But they will wait in a position called questing, where they find the tall tips of grasses or shrubs. They use their third and fourth pairs of legs to hold on to the grass or leaves and outstretch their front legs, ready to climb onto a host. When a host passes by and brushes against the grass or shrub where the tick is waiting, it quickly climbs aboard. Once on their hosts, some ticks will attach themselves immediately, while others will look around on their hosts and seek a place where the skin is thinner and the blood is easier to access, such as the ears, armpits, or scalp.

From Tick to Host

How does a tick transmit a pathogen—a virus or bacteria that can cause disease—once it has found a host? The tick must prepare to feed on its host. Depending on where it is in its life cycle, this could take anywhere from ten minutes to two hours. Once it decides on the spot where it wants to feed, the tick will grasp the skin of its host and cut into it, using its mouthparts. Then the tick inserts its feeding tube. This tube also has barbs that help it stay in place while the tick feeds. In addition, it can secrete a substance that acts a little like cement, keeping the tube in the cut. This substance also thins the host's blood, numbs its skin, and fights the host's immune system response. The numbing property helps keep the host from feeling or noticing the tick's bite. Also, ticks like to hide in places like armpits and scalps, making them more difficult to see. And because people are often bitten by ticks in the nymph stage, when they are less than 2 millimeters long, they are even more difficult to spot. Nymphs are most active during the spring and summer months, when people are also more likely to be outside.

The tick will remain in place for two to three days. It will swell up to twice its size on ingested blood. If the host person or animal has any pathogens in its blood, the tick will ingest those as well. And because small amounts of the tick's saliva enter through the host's skin, any pathogen that the tick carries is transferred to the host. In most cases, the tick must remain attached for thirty-six to forty-eight hours in order to transmit a pathogen. Soft-bodied ticks finish feeding more quickly than hard-bodied ticks. If they are not discovered, both types will drop off the host once they are engorged and full of blood. A female tick that has fed fully on a host may weigh 120 to 150 times more after feeding than she did before!

More Predators, Please

Scientists believe that some of the increase in tick populations that carry Lyme disease is due to the loss of predators like foxes, weasels, fishers, and stone martens. These predators have been hunted. Their numbers have also been reduced because of a loss of habitat.

Ticks like to feed on white-footed mice and can then transfer to humans and other animals. In a study by Tim R. Hofmeester, described in the article "Lyme Disease's Worst Enemy? It Might Be Foxes," by Amy Harmon, he tested the numbers of ticks on white-footed mice in the Dutch countryside. He

(continued on the next page)

Predators like this red fox are declining in numbers. These animals hunt prey like white-footed mice, which are very likely to carry ticks. Fewer predators mean more mice and more ticks.

(continued from the previous page)

found that in areas where foxes and other mouse predators were protected, only 10 to 20 percent of newly hatched ticks were on the mice. In areas with high numbers of ticks, it might be a good idea to protect predators like foxes. This could help reduce the populations of mice carrying infected ticks.

A Variety of Diseases

Ticks transfer pathogens in basically the same way, no matter what kind of tick they are. But there are many diseases that humans can get from these pathogens.

Lyme disease is one of the best-known tick-borne diseases. It is caused by the bacterium *Borrelia burgdorferi*. It is transmitted by the bite of infected black-legged ticks, also known as deer ticks. The symptoms of Lyme disease include the recognizable bull's-eye skin rash, as well as headache, fever, swollen lymph nodes, and fatigue. If it is not diagnosed or treated, it can damage joints, the heart, and the nervous system and even cause memory loss. It is treated in the early stages with several types of antibiotics. This medicine can be taken orally or intravenously if the symptoms are severe.

Anaplasmosis is caused by the bacterium *Anaplasma phagocytophilum*, spread by the bites of black-legged and western black-legged ticks. The tick bite is painless and most people don't even realize they've been bitten. Symptoms begin one to two weeks after the bite. Early symptoms include fever, chills, muscle aches, vomiting and nausea, and severe headaches. If not treated, it can lead to respiratory and organ failure, bleeding, and death. It is usually treated with the antibiotic doxycycline.

Rocky Mountain spotted fever (RMSF) can be transmitted by the American dog tick, the Rocky Mountain wood tick, and the brown dog tick. RMSF is one of several diseases caused by the bacteria *rickettsia*. RMSF is the most severe and can cause death if it is not treated. The rash can look like red splotches or small, spotted dots and develops two to four days after the fever begins. Patients who have severe cases of RMSF may end up having to have fingers, toes, arms, or even legs amputated because of damage to the blood vessels in those areas. They may also suffer from hearing loss, paralysis, or mental disabilities. If caught early, it can be successfully treated with doxycycline.

Tularemia, or rabbit fever, can be found few places. One such place is the island of Martha's Vineyard, off the coast of Massachusetts. The disease was brought to the island when rabbits from Arkansas, one of the other places in the United States where tularemia is found, were introduced by humans in the 1930s. Tularemia can be found in six different forms on the island. At first, the pneumonic form of the disease commonly infected people. This affected people's lungs. It happened because the bacteria that causes tularemia became airborne, usually from a dead or dying infected animal. According to Julia Wells in her article "After Tularemia Death, Experts Stress Education," in the *Vineyard Gazette*, now, however,

Martha's Vineyard is one of the few places where the tick-borne illness tularemia occurs. The disease was accidentally introduced in the 1930s when rabbits were brought ashore.

the tick-borne form is becoming more common. It is being transmitted by dog ticks and lone star ticks. Lone star ticks are new to the island. In August 2018, a Martha's Vineyard resident died from tularemia after clearing brush on his property.

Ticks and Dinosaurs?

It may sound like something from a *Jurassic Park* movie, but researchers have recently discovered that ticks were feeding on dinosaurs ninety-nine million years ago! According to the article "99-Million-Year-Old Amber Contains First Evidence That Ticks Fed on Dinosaurs," published by the American Museum of Natural History,

Researchers discovered that ticks were most likely feeding on dinosaurs, perhaps like this T. Rex, millions of years ago. Fossils of ticks attached to the feathers of theropod dinosaurs have been found.

researchers found a fossil record in a piece of Burmese amber, which contained a hard tick clinging to a feather. They knew that the feather did not belong to a modern bird but instead to a theropod dinosaur. Researchers have also found other evidence of ticks feeding on theropods, such as a newly identified species of extinct tick named *Deinocroton draculi*, or "Dracula's terrible tick," which was also preserved in amber. It dated to the Cretaceous period (145 to 166 million years ago). Researchers think that these ticks may have lived in the nests of feathered dinosaurs.

Babesiosis is a disease caused by microscopic parasites that infect red blood cells. Most cases of babesiosis in the United States are caused by the parasite *Babesia microti*. *Babesia microti* is transmitted by the black-legged tick. The nymph stage of the tick, during which it is about the size of a poppy seed, usually transmits the disease. Most people who are infected never develop any symptoms of the disease and do not need treatment.

But some people develop flu-like symptoms, such as fever, chills, sweats, headache, body aches, loss of appetite, nausea, or fatigue. Because the disease infects the red blood cells, it can also destroy them and cause anemia. Babesiosis can be life-threatening to people with compromised immune systems, the elderly, or those who already have serious diseases. The only way to diagnose it is by blood tests to check red blood cells under a microscope.

Powassan virus can be transmitted by the black-legged tick and the groundhog tick. These ticks are mostly found in the Northeast and Great Lakes regions of the United States. It used to be considered rare, but the number of cases is growing. Some people never experience any effects from it. But Powassan virus can be severe. People who develop it must sometimes be hospitalized to help them breathe and because of brain swelling. The virus can infect the central nervous system and cause encephalitis (inflammation of the brain) and meningitis (inflammation of the membranes that surround the brain and spinal cord). Many people who recover from Powassan virus have permanent memory problems, severe recurring headaches, and muscle loss. In 10 percent of cases, it can be fatal.

These are just a few of the many illnesses that can be caused by the bite of an infected tick. Tick-borne illnesses can range from so slight that the infected person never even knows he or she has the disease, to so severe that they cause permanent effects or even death. Tick illnesses are not new to humans, but they are a serious problem, and scientists are wondering why they seem to be getting worse.

Myths & FACTS

Myth: You can get Lyme disease only if you live in a few areas of the United States.

Fact: Lyme disease has been reported in every state in the United States.

Myth: Ticks often fall out of trees and land on people who are walking below.

Fact: Ticks look for meals close to the ground, to make it easy to attach themselves to rodents and mice. The highest they climb is into shrubs and bushes. This is so they can attach to larger mammals.

Myth: The best way to detach a tick that has bitten you is to use a lit match, cover it with nail polish, or dab it with alcohol.

Fact: The best way to detach a tick that is imbedded in your skin is with tweezers. Other methods require leaving the tick in place for a longer time, which gives it time to transmit an infection.

CHAPTER THREE

A Serious Problem

Scientists have been studying ticks since 1893, when Theobald Smith and Frederick Kilbourne discovered that ticks transmitted Texas cattle fever. At the beginning of the twentieth century, scientists made the connection between ticks and human illnesses. In 1905, scientists discovered tick-relapsing fever, transmitted by the soft-bodied tick *Ornithodoros moubata.* In the spring of 1906, scientist Howard Taylor Ricketts began studying Rocky Mountain spotted fever. At that time, all he knew was that the disease occurred in a very specific sections of the Rocky Mountains, on its western slopes, and primarily in the spring. He also knew there was a mortality rate ranging widely between 5 percent and 90 percent, depending on where the victim lived.

Specific areas of the Rocky Mountains, especially the western slopes, are where Rocky Mountain spotted fever was first identified. The disease is caused by infected tick bites.

Tick Science at Work

Ricketts went to Montana and spent four years studying the disease and the possibility that it was carried by ticks. According to the article "What a Revelation Any Science Is!" in the *American Society for Microbiology*, by Lynn Margulis and Betsy Palmer Eldridge:

Scientist Howard Taylor Ricketts spent four years studying Rocky Mountain spotted fever. He discovered the bacterium that causes the disease.

> *[He] set up a 14-by-14-foot tent in the hospital yard in which he slept (under army blankets, since it was cold) and which he also used as a laboratory. In the course of these studies in Montana, Ricketts made extensive collections of local ticks in the Bitteroot Valley and designed tick cages to better observe the "bipolar bacilli." He aligned the caged and labeled ticks in rows. Working mostly alone and separated from his young family, he oversaw every aspect of the field and laboratory project.*

Not long after arriving in Montana, Ricketts studied the case of a ten-year-old boy named William Robert Landon, his father (a farmer), and his family.

Ricketts noted that the family drank water from a nearby creek and irrigation ditches. They did not boil it before drinking it. He also wrote about the family's exposure to insects, especially in the spring after the snow melted:

> *Ticks are around the house, on trees, on ground, everywhere. Every body bitten innumerable times. Mosquitoes most numerous in July. Has seen a few this spring. Has not been bitten [by mosquitoes], nor has boy. Boy has been bitten many times by ticks.*

Ricketts took a blood sample from the boy. He discovered a bacterium that he believed was causing Rocky Mountain spotted fever. The bacterium was named *Rickettsia rickettsia*, after H. T. Ricketts. He proved the cause of the fever by experimenting on guinea pigs. The guinea pigs were injected with blood from a human suffering from the fever. They were also exposed to infected ticks. Sadly, Ricketts died of typhus fever in Mexico in 1910. He was there studying how that disease was transmitted.

Tick Collecting

Just how do scientists find and collect ticks in order to study them? They use a method called flagging, or dragging. They stretch a cloth or a blanket over vegetation, such as bushes or shrubs. The ticks become attached to it and can then be removed. Because ticks are attracted to the carbon dioxide that breathing animals give off, scientist sometimes use a carbon dioxide trap. They do this by using dry ice to create carbon dioxide. It is placed in a perforated container in the middle of a square of cloth. The ticks are attracted to it and

(continued on the next page)

Pets, especially dogs, are common tick carriers. Ticks hide in the animals' coats, and dog owners must check their pets for ticks anytime they have been outside and carefully remove them if found.

(continued from the previous page)

become trapped. Ticks can also be collected from the nests and burrows of animal hosts or from the animals themselves. They can be removed with forceps.

Tick Study Continues

Throughout the early twentieth century, and following World War II, scientists continued to discover the links between certain types of ticks and certain illnesses. Scientists have learned that Lyme disease is the most health-threatening disease carried by vectors like ticks. This is true in both the United States and Europe. However, more tick-borne infections and bacteria are constantly being found around the world.

Scientists are discovering that ticks don't just carry bacteria that cause illnesses in both people and animals. Ticks are also becoming reservoirs—storage places—for tick-transmitted bacteria. Ticks are maintaining and transferring the bacteria from stage to stage of their own life cycles. They are also keeping the bacteria from one generation to the next through the eggs that are carried by an infected female tick. And because every species of tick has its optimum geographic location in terms of climate and geography, people and animals in these areas are at high risk. This is not only because the ticks carry and transmit the bacteria but also because they are storing the bacteria in their bodies.

Scientists are continuing to find new tick-borne diseases in the United States, and the diseases are spreading. Between 1969 and 2014, eleven new diseases caused by tick bites were identified. Some of them, like anaplasmosis, ehrlichiosis, and babesiosis, are causing thousands of cases of illness each year. According to ecologist Felicia Keesing, quoted in the NPR article "Beyond Lyme: New Tick-borne Diseases on the rise in U.S.," by Micaheleen Doucleff and Jane Greenhalgh, "The more we look [for tick-borne viruses], in a sense, the more we find."

- **The Northeast** sees anaplasmosis, babesiosis, and a new bacterium related to Lyme disease.
- **The Midwest** now sees another new Lyme-type virus called the Heartland virus, as well as the Bourbon virus.

The Statistics

In May 2018, the CDC released the results of a study entitled "Trends in Reported Vectorborne Disease Cases—United States and Territories, 2004–2016." "Vectorborne" refers to diseases that are transmitted by ticks, mosquitoes, or fleas. Key findings from the report included:

- Tick-borne diseases more than doubled in thirteen years and were 77 percent of all

The Centers for Disease Control and Prevention (CDC) track outbreaks of tick-borne illnesses by type and location. They study these illnesses and provide information to the public.

vectorborne disease reports. Lyme disease accounted for 82 percent of all tick-borne cases, but spotted fever, rickettsioses, babesiosis, and anaplasmosis/ehrlichiosis cases also increased.

- During 2004 to 2016, nine vectorborne human diseases were reported for the first time from the United States and US territories.
- Vectorborne diseases have been difficult to prevent and control. Many of the vectorborne diseases including Lyme disease and West Nile virus (from mosquitoes) have animal reservoirs. Insecticide resistance is widespread and increasing.

- **The South** sees southern tick-associated rash illness.
- **The West** is seeing a new type of spotted fever.

And all over the country people are contracting ehrlichiosis. Many of the new diseases are still rare. But these diseases are causing serious concern to scientists and doctors, such as the Powassan virus.

Tucker Lane of Barnstable, Massachusetts, was used to tick bites. Ticks were very common where he lives on Cape Cod. But after two tick bites one summer, he contracted the Powassan virus. "I just had a pounding headache. I was sweating but was cold. And I had tremors," Lane told researchers in the article "Beyond Lyme: New Tick-borne Diseases on the rise in U.S.," for NPR. He developed projectile vomiting, a high fever, and double vision. His mother called an ambulance, and he was rushed to the hospital, where he soon fell into a coma. Tests showed that he had inflammation deep inside his brain. Lane ended up on life support in the intensive care unit, just a few days after he first got a headache. But he slowly began to get better on his own, and his doctors are still not sure why. Another person who contracted Powassan virus, a woman who was bitten by a tick in Maine, was not so fortunate. "She subsequently went downhill, so unbelievably quickly," her daughter said. "She became incoherent and delusional. She was talking to paintings." She died after being placed on life support and becoming unresponsive.

Researchers have also discovered that some people may end up with more than one tick-borne pathogen, which is called coinfection. Ticks that contain more than one type of pathogen can transmit multiple pathogens with just one bite. Some tick-borne diseases can also be transmitted without a tick bite, from one infected person to another, usually through a blood transfusion, an organ transplant, or from a pregnant mother to her fetus. People who end up with coinfections may be infected both acutely (having an active disease or illness) or chronically (an illness or infection that will periodically cause illness but sometimes become inactive). Doctors have found that people who have frequent symptoms of a tick-borne illness may actually have more than one disease. These people end up being chronically ill, which makes them less productive at home and at work. They can also be more likely to die.

Where Ticks Live

Tick-borne illnesses are not just on the rise in the United States. They can be found all over the world.

Lyme disease is present in forty-five countries, from Canada and the United States to Europe and Asia.

Tick-borne encephalitis (TBE), which causes fever, headache, fatigue, muscle pain, nausea, and loss of appetite, is found in thirty countries. TBE is found mostly in Asia and Europe. Peak transmission time is May through November. Travelers are advised to get the TBE vaccine before traveling to these countries.

Tick-borne spotted fever is any illness caused by ticks carrying the rickettsia bacteria. It is difficult to diagnose because not everyone will have symptoms. In the United States, Mexico, and Panama, it is called Rocky Mountain spotted fever. In sub-Saharan Africa, it is called African tick-bite fever. People who go on safari trips are often at risk of contracting this fever.

Crimean-Congo hemorrhagic fever (CCHF) is found in southern and eastern Europe, central Asia, Africa, Southeast Asia, and the Middle East. People who come in close contact with animals are especially at risk because CCHF affects wild animals and livestock. Humans become ill when they are bitten by infected ticks. They can also get sick if they come into contact with infected animal blood or tissues.

Mouse Tick Assassins?

As scientists look for ways to kill ticks, they have found a strange secret weapon: white-footed mice. These mice are always covered in ticks, and for some unknown reason, they don't groom them off like other animals do. They let them stay attached and bite. They can be covered with as many as one hundred ticks at a time. These ticks

(continued on the next page)

The white-footed mouse is one of the biggest carriers of ticks. One may carry as many as one hundred ticks on its body at a time. Scientists don't know why these mice don't groom the ticks off.

(continued from the previous page)

have been tested and often carry many pathogens at once. Scientists are experimenting with creating traps where these mice like to hide. They place a little brush that applies a drop of insecticide on the mouse's back any time it enters the trap. For weeks following the application, these mice will kill any ticks that land on them, making the mice tiny tick assassins.

Ticks are all around us, in every part of the world, and the incidence of tick-borne illnesses and the discoveries of new illnesses are growing. It may seem like it is impossible to defend our health against such tiny and often deadly carriers of viruses. But there are precautions and treatments that will help. And as the threat grows, it is more important than ever to learn what can be done to defend against ticks and stay healthy.

CHAPTER FOUR

Tick-Bite Triage

Ticks are everywhere, found in almost every part of the world, and their numbers are increasing rapidly. Chances are most people will experience a tick bite at some point. And because the risk of getting a tick-borne illness is increasing, it is important to know what to look for, how to remove ticks when they do bite, and what to look for after a bite.

Be Prepared

The first step in dealing with tick bites is prevention. Before you even step foot outside, you should pay attention to where you are going. Ticks like grassy areas or areas with brush and woods. Most people get bitten by ticks in their own backyards or in their neighborhoods. But anyone who spends time camping, hunting, or gardening could potentially encounter ticks. When outside, you should avoid sitting on the grass or on a stone wall, as this makes it easy for ticks to jump onto skin and clothing.

Landscaping Tips

One way to limit the number of ticks living in a backyard is good landscaping and lawn upkeep. Ticks need humidity and shade to survive. They will avoid neatly tended, close-trimmed lawns in the full sun because there won't be enough shade and moisture. Most backyard ticks are found close to the edges of a lawn—82 percent of deer ticks are found within 9 feet (3 meters) of the edges of lawns, according to the article "13 Secrets Ticks Won't Tell You to Avoid Getting Bitten," by Lauren Gelman—so borders of bark mulch, wood chips, or gravel will keep them from migrating onto a lawn. People whose lawns are shady should thin their trees to allow more sunshine in, and shrubs should be trimmed. It also helps to clean up any piles of brush and pull any weeds. This not only keeps ticks away but also leaves fewer hiding places for white-footed mice, one of the biggest carriers of ticks.

Repellent 101

Anyone who is going outside in an area with tick infestations should be prepared. The CDC suggests first using an insect repellent on clothing, footwear, and gear. It should contain permethrin, which will last through several washings. Permethrin-treated clothing, socks, and boots can also be purchased. Permethrin comes from the pyrethroid family of synthetic chemicals. It mimics the natural extracts from chrysanthemum flowers. If insects eat it or touch it, it causes muscle spasms, paralysis, and death. This is because insect bodies cannot break it down quickly. It is not as toxic to humans or dogs because their bodies can break it down more quickly, although cats are more susceptible to it.

Humans should also use insect repellent on their skin. The CDC recommends repellents containing DEET, picaridin, IR3535, oil of lemon eucalyptus (OLE), para-menthane-diol (PMD), or 2-undecanone. However, babies under two months should not wear insect repellents, and children

It is very important to use insect repellent on any exposed skin to help prevent tick bites. It is also best to wear long pants and long sleeves when going outside in tick-prone areas.

younger than three should not wear products containing OLE or PMD.

It can be hard to find out which repellent is the best one to use, depending on the age of the user, the type of insects you are trying to avoid, and what is safe. The US Environmental Protection Agency (EPA) has created an interactive website, "Find the Repellent That Is Right for You" at https://www.epa.gov/insect-repellents/find-repellent-right-you. A doctor or pharmacist can also recommend the best repellent.

Dress for Success

In addition to treating clothing and skin with insecticides and repellents, it is also important to wear appropriate clothing in an appropriate way.

Clothing should be light colored, to make it easier to spot a tick. Bare skin should be minimized by wearing long-sleeved shirts and pants instead of shorts. Pants should be tucked into socks so that ticks can't climb up inside pant legs.

Tick Hide and Seek

When returning inside after being in a tick-prone area, take off your clothing right away and check it for ticks. According to the CDC:

- Remove any ticks and wash clothes or put them in the dryer if damp. Tumble dry clothes in a dryer on high heat for ten minutes to kill ticks on dry clothing after you come indoors. If the clothes are damp, you may need to dry them longer.
- When washing clothes first, use hot water. Cold and medium-temperature water will not kill ticks effectively.

The most important thing for anyone to do is to check his or her body for any ticks. Ticks love to hide in places where it is difficult to see them, and a mirror may be required to do a thorough check.

Parents should always check children after they have been outside. Ticks can attach themselves anywhere on the human body, but they especially like warm, moist places like the groin and armpits. Ticks that attach themselves to pant legs or shirt sleeves will crawl up the body to these places. They should be the first places checked. Ticks also like the back of the knees and inside the belly button, as well as hair, including the hair on the head as well as beards. They will hide on the scalp or the back of the neck. On both humans and pets, ticks also like to attach behind and around the ears.

Down, Doggy

Pets, especially dogs, usually carry ticks. Researchers have found that people who have dogs or cats that go outside have twice the risk of contracting a tick-borne disease as do people without pets. According to data collected by the CDC, 31 percent of pet owners had found a tick crawling on a human member of the household, and 19 percent found a tick actually attached to a human in the household.

Ticks that are brought inside by pets can not only attach themselves to that pet but can also attach to a nearby human. Pet owners must check their pets thoroughly when they come inside. Then they must check themselves. In animals, ticks are especially fond of hiding in between the toes on the animal's paws. Other places where ticks hide are in and

Dogs love to run in tall grass and wooded areas. Therefore, they must be carefully checked for ticks, as ticks can hide in many places on a dog's body.

around the ears, under the animal's collar, around its tail, under the front legs, between the back legs, and around the eyelids.

Pets can also be treated with anti–tick and flea medications or with chemically infused collars, but it is important that only vet-approved repellents be used with any pet. Cats in particular are very sensitive to certain insect repellent products. Pets are another reason why the areas they usually spend time in outside, such as a backyard, should be maintained in a way that makes them less tick-friendly habitats.

Taking Off Ticks

What is the best way to remove a tick from a human or a pet once it has been found? There are some specialized tick-removal devices one can buy, but the best method is to use a pair of tweezers. According to the CDC:

- Use fine-tipped tweezers to grasp the tick as close to the skin's surface as possible.
- Pull upward with steady, even pressure. Don't twist or jerk the tick; this can cause the

mouthparts to break off and remain in the skin. If this happens, remove the mouthparts with tweezers. If you are unable to remove the mouthparts easily with clean tweezers, leave them alone and let the skin heal.

- After removing the tick, thoroughly clean the bite area and your hands with rubbing alcohol or soap and water.
- Never crush a tick with your fingers. Dispose of a live tick by putting it in alcohol, placing it in a sealed bag or container, wrapping it tightly in tape, or flushing it down the toilet.

Avoid folklore remedies such as "painting" the tick with nail polish or petroleum jelly or using heat to make the tick detach from the skin. Your goal is to remove the tick as quickly as possible—not to wait for it to detach.

Removing ticks from pets is a similar process but is more difficult because animals get nervous or anxious when they're being prodded and poked. It usually requires a second person to hold the animal and keep it calm. The person removing the tick should wear gloves. Never crush the tick after removal because it could spread infectious fluids. The tick is removed in the same way as on a person, but if the owner suspects that some of the tick's mouthparts might have remained in the animal's skin, then he or she must bring the animal to the vet

To Test or Not to Test

Some people who find and remove a tick from themselves then wonder if they should have that tick tested for infection. Some commercial companies offer tick testing, but the CDC does not recommend having it done. Some laboratories do not have the same standards that clinical diagnostic labs have, and their results might not be accurate. And just because a tick tests positive for an infection does not mean that it transmitted that infection when it bit you. On the other hand, a false negative might make that person think he or she is fine, and he or she won't be looking for symptoms of a tick-borne illness. Finally, symptoms might develop before the testing results are even returned from a lab.

to have the rest removed. The removed tick should be killed by putting it in a jar of rubbing alcohol, but it should be kept in case the pet begins to show symptoms of a disease.

Diagnosing a Tick-Borne Illness

Tick-borne illnesses differ from each other in severity and symptoms, but they all have some similarities in common: fever and chills; headaches; fatigue; muscle aches; and rashes in different shapes, sizes, and colors. There is even a form of tick-borne paralysis, which is rare and is thought to be caused by a toxin in tick saliva. It creates a type of paralysis in the victim—usually children—which usually goes away within twenty-four hours of removing the tick. If any of these symptoms develop within a few weeks of having been bitten by a tick, it is important to see a doctor for a diagnosis. Many tick-borne illnesses can be successfully treated if they are caught in time, but they can have long-term health effects or even result in death if they are not diagnosed and treated quickly. The doctor will evaluate the symptoms, as

It is important to see a doctor as soon as any symptoms develop that could be related to a tick bite. Many tick-borne illnesses can have long-term effects if they aren't treated right away.

well as the geographic region where the bite took place, since this can help determine what the illness is based on what ticks and tick infections are present there.

Illnesses caused by tick bites are usually diagnosed by examination of rashes and other symptoms, and then in some cases by a blood test. The problem is that ticks can cause more than one disease in a human host at a time, but these illnesses have to be tested for separately. Diseases like Lyme disease and ehrlichiosis can be tested for using a blood test, but the timing of the test is important. If testing takes place too soon, before several weeks have passed, it may show a false negative, before the infection and its symptoms have developed. In February 2018, researchers at the Columbia University Mailman School of Public Health released findings on existing tests in the article "First Multiplex Test for Tick-Borne Diseases":

> *Currently, diagnosis of Lyme disease, the most common TBD, requires two separate tests. This cumbersome approach also relies on subjective criteria for the interpretation of results, and accurately identifies fewer than 40 percent of patients with early disease and results in false positives in 28 percent of the time. The accuracy of the method used to diagnose TBDs Babesia, Anaplasma, Ehrlichia, and Rickettsia varies widely among testing laboratories. And for other tick-borne agents, specific blood tests are not yet available, or in the case of the potentially*

deadly Powassan virus or Heartland virus, are only performed in specialized laboratories.

They also released information about the development of a new blood test. This test could check for multiple tick-borne illnesses at the same time. The new blood test, called the Tick-Borne Disease Serochip (TBD Serochip) test, can test for eight tick-borne illnesses at the same time. It can also test whether a single individual is infected with more than one illness. Researchers hope that the test will be available to the general public in 2019.

Once a patient has been diagnosed with a tick-borne illness, he or she is usually treated with some kind of antibiotic, depending on the illness. In extreme cases, he or she may need to be hospitalized.

Cure or Danger?

In 2006, the Food and Drug Administration (FDA) issued a warning against a product called bismacine, also known as chromocene. It was sold as an alternative treatment for Lyme disease and was injected directly into patients. Because it was not approved by the FDA, it had to be prescribed or administered by "alternative health" doctors. Bismacine contained high amounts of bismuth, a heavy metal that is used in some medications but is not approved for injection. Bismuth caused side effects including cardiovascular collapse and kidney failure. At least one person died after receiving bismacine treatment, and others were hospitalized. The FDA urged patients not to take the medication and to seek medical help if they had.

Meat Allergies

One of the more unusual illnesses that can be transmitted by a tick bite is an allergy to meat, such as beef or pork. This can happen to people who have been eating meat without problem for their entire lives. People bitten by the lone star tick can develop high levels of alpha-gal, a sugar molecule, in their blood. This triggers an immune system reaction whenever they eat red meat, which can cause symptoms such as hives; itching or itchy, scaly skin (eczema); swelling of

(continued on the next page)

(continued from the previous page)

the lips, face, tongue, throat, or other body parts; wheezing or shortness of breath; runny nose; abdominal pain; diarrhea; nausea or vomiting; sneezing; and headaches. Its most severe effects are symptoms of anaphylactic shock, which causes difficulty breathing, similar to the allergic reactions people get from eating shellfish or peanuts. There is no cure, and sufferers must avoid eating meat or meat-based products and usually carry emergency epinephrine injections to treat unexpected episodes of anaphylactic shock.

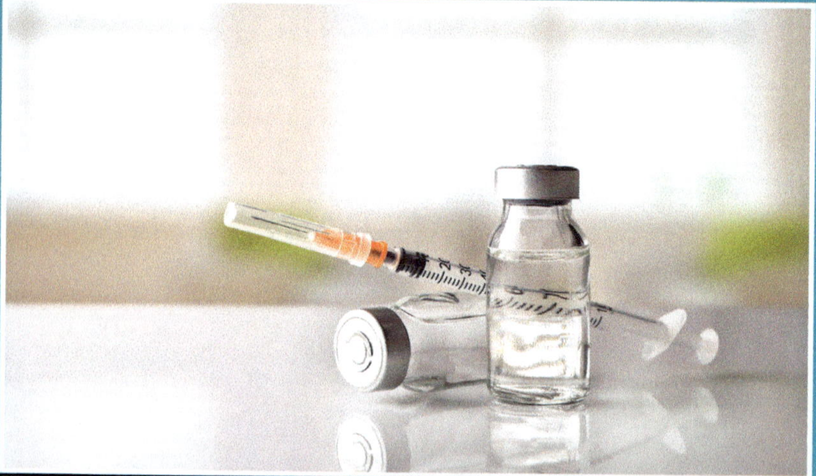

Scientists are trying to develop effective and safe vaccines for tick-borne illnesses. However, it is not easy to find funding for research because other illnesses take priority.

Possible Vaccine

Scientists have been working on the development of vaccines for tick-borne illnesses. In 1998, a vaccine called LYMErix was approved by the US Food and Drug Administration for use by people aged fifteen to seventy in regions where Lyme disease was common. However, there were complaints and lawsuits by some of the people who received the vaccine because of side effects such as arthritis, and the vaccine was pulled off the market. However, a new vaccine has just passed safety trials. It is similar to LYMErix but also protects against additional tick species that are known to cause Lyme disease in people, including those in Europe. No release date for the vaccine is available.

There is no denying the statistics: tick-borne illnesses are increasing around the world. Have they reached epidemic scale? And what can be done to combat these microscopic pathogens and their vectors?

10 Great Questions to Ask a Doctor

1. Can I get a tick bite even if I never go into the woods?
2. How long does a tick need to be attached to me in order to transmit a disease?
3. Can I get Lyme disease even if I don't have the classic bull's-eye-shaped rash?
4. Can I get a tick-borne illness even if I don't remember being bitten by a tick?
5. Should I wait until a lab test comes back positive before I start taking antibiotics for a tick-borne illness?
6. Can I get a tick bite only during the summer months?
7. Can I use a natural insect repellent to keep ticks away?
8. If a tick bites me and I remove it, should I have it tested by a laboratory?
9. Do ticks always transmit a disease when they bite a human or animal?
10. What kinds of ticks are found in my area, and which ones are dangerous?

CHAPTER FIVE

Dealing with an Epidemic

Diseases caused by ticks, fleas, and mosquitoes have been around for as long as there have been humans, and in some cases, even before. However, many people, especially those who grew up thirty or forty years ago, never encountered illnesses like Lyme disease or anaplasmosis or Rocky Mountain spotted fever. They aren't used to protecting themselves against ticks. However, as tick-borne illnesses increase, the need to adjust outdoor lifestyles to accommodate the presence of ticks and other vectors is becoming more and more important.

On the Rise

According to a study released by the CDC in May 2018, illnesses spread by tick, flea, and mosquito bites tripled from 2004 to 2016. During this time, 640,000 cases of vector-borne diseases were reported in the United States. Also during that time, nine new illnesses spread by mosquitoes and ticks have been discovered or introduced into the United States, and seven of them were carried by ticks. "Zika, West Nile, Lyme, and chikungunya—a growing list of diseases caused by the bite of an infected mosquito, tick, or flea—have confronted the U.S. in recent years, making a lot of people sick.

Diseases caused by vectors like mosquitoes and ticks are becoming more common. This poster urges people to use mosquito repellent to prevent bites that transmit the Zika virus.

And we don't know what will threaten Americans next," said CDC director Dr. Robert R. Redfield in a report on the CDC website. Tick-borne diseases alone tripled during the thirteen years of the study and accounted for more than 60 percent of all the vector-borne diseases reported. And because ticks are found all across the United States, and their range is expanding, the chances of encountering ticks that carry disease are also increasing.

A Local Epidemic

On Long Island, New York, the incidence of tick-borne Lyme disease has bordered on an epidemic, especially among children. Jorge Benach, a molecular geneticist at Stony Brook University School of Medicine, said in a *Newsday* article by Delthia Hicks, "Lyme disease is mostly a disease of children and curiously mostly a disease of boys." New York State has the highest number of confirmed cases of Lyme disease in the country, with ninety-five thousand cases since 1996, and Long Island, particularly Suffolk County, has the highest rates because it has the most dense concentration of ticks.

Vector-borne diseases are not just a problem in the United States, where the risk from these diseases is increasing. They are a major cause of illness and death all around the world, and most countries are not prepared for the increase in these diseases. Causes for the increase include warmer global temperatures that enable ticks to thrive in new areas, a lack of vaccines for many tick illnesses, and international jet travel. Some of the tick-borne illnesses in the United States have been introduced from other countries through ticks that have been inadvertently carried by travelers. Almost every place in the world has ticks of one kind or another, and they carry different diseases. Some central European countries, including Austria, the Czech Republic, Germany, and Slovenia, have high incidence of tick-borne encephalitis, which can be fatal. Slovenia experiences an even more dangerous type of tick-borne encephalitis.

The Cost of Tick-Borne Illnesses

Tick-borne illnesses can have a very high price in terms of the health and well-being of individuals and families. But they also have an economic impact as well. In 2015, the cost of diagnosing and treating patients with Lyme disease in particular had already reached between $712 million and $1.3 billion a year for the US health care system—or on average about $3,000 per patient—for an estimated 240,000 to 440,000 new cases of the tick-borne illness diagnosed every year. This included the initial testing for diagnosis, treatment, and then returning visits for additional care if symptoms had not subsided. "Our study looks at the actual costs of treating patients in the year following their Lyme diagnosis," says study author Emily Adrion on the Johns Hopkins Bloomberg School of Public Health website. People who are diagnosed with Lyme disease return to the doctor with the same symptoms. They are retested and often retreated. This costs the health care system a great deal of money—about $1 billion per year. Adion says, "It is clear that we need effective, cost-effective and compassionate management of these patients to improve their outcomes even if we don't know what to call the disease."

But cost is not limited to the dollars spent on health care and prevention alone. There is also a cost in terms of time spent outdoors engaging in recreation. In 2017, according to an article by Kevin Berry, Jude Bayham, Spencer R. Meyer, and Eli P. Fenichel, "The Allocation of Time and Risk of Lyme: A Case of Ecosystem Service Income and Substitution Effects," in the journal *Environmental and Resource Economics*, the fear of contracting Lyme disease among people in the Northeast United States has cost about nine hours of lost time outdoors per person, which equals a total cost of roughly $2.8 billion to $5 billion annually in lost trips, due to the large number of people in the region. This not only impacts the individual but also the tourist economies of the regions where they would have traveled and spent money. According to Eli Fenichel, one of the article's authors:

> *Lyme disease has been around for a few decades but it still has a big cost to society. But the cost is not what people spend on doctors, or medicine, or even bug spray. These are costs that everybody incurs because we're all choosing second-choice activities to avoid getting Lyme disease. It's a lot of people making*

very small changes, but in such a densely populated region that has major impacts.

Ticks and Livestock

Ticks can have a devastating effect on farmers when their livestock becomes infected by ticks. Costs include the price of treating the infected animals (or the loss of livestock if the infection leads to the animal's death), as well as the loss of milk, meat, or other commodities that farmers sell on the agricultural market. This affects not only US farmers but also farmers in places such as India and Africa, where ticks are even more common. In India, almost all livestock suffers from tick infestation. Farmers there lose approximately $275.7 million (in US dollars) annually because of tick illnesses in their cattle, which reduces the amount of milk produced and requires farmers to spend money on tick control. In Tanzania, Africa, tick-borne diseases, including anaplasmosis, babesiosis, cowdriosis, and theileriosis, cost farmers $364 million US in production losses and treatment and control costs,

Ticks can hurt the agricultural economy. Farmers lose money when cattle become infected by ticks, get sick, and require veterinary treatment.

including the death of about 1.3 million cattle. In developing countries especially, there are few resources for managing tick infestations and illnesses. Veterinary costs increase, and the infected animals reproduce at a lower rate, all of which harm the farm economy.

Closer to home, in Texas, cattle fever ticks that carry the blood disease babesiosis, which once nearly destroyed the Texas cattle industry, have started to move north out of a tick quarantine zone. This zone, established by the US Department of Agriculture, required inspection and quarantine of infected cattle through a system of "tick riders" who patrolled the zone in search of stray cattle and horses as well as any wildlife that might also carry

In Texas, there are so many ticks that special "tick riders" patrol for stray animals that may carry them. Ticks cost the Texas cattle industry millions of dollars each year.

ticks. Despite these efforts, which helped control the tick population, in 2017 these ticks had moved north in large numbers. Ranches where evidence of the ticks are found are quarantined, and ranchers must inspect their cattle and use tick repellents on their herds. Ranchers and the government are trying to prevent another outbreak of Texas cattle fever, which would cost an estimated $123 million in the first year of an outbreak. Annual costs for similar-sized outbreaks would be about $97 million.

Looking to the Future

Tick-borne diseases are becoming more common around the world, and scientists and medical professionals are beginning to pay more attention to them as a result. With environmental changes like climate change, increasing population growth, settlement encroaching on formerly wild areas bring people into closer contact with wildlife, and the ability of jet transportation to bring people (and ticks) quickly from one place to another around the world, some researchers feel that tick-borne illnesses will pose a greater overall health danger in the near future. This danger could be greater than epidemics like Ebola, SARS, and Zika, which have received a great deal of media attention. As zoologist Mackenzie Kwak states in the *Guardian* article "Forget Ebola, Sars and Zika: ticks are the next global health threat":

> *Since the beginning of our species we have been at war. It's a continuous, neverending fight against the smallest of adversaries: armies of pathogens and parasites. As we have developed new ways to survive and stop them, they have evolved ever more complex and ingenious methods to thwart our efforts.*

Because of the increasing number of ticks all over the world and lack of success at creating effective vaccines for many tick-borne illnesses, ticks could very well be the source of the next great human epidemic.

In order to try and prevent tick-borne illness outbreaks, the CDC has issued a series of

Cattle Ticks

According to an article in Southwest FarmPress by Logan Hawkes:

To understand how quickly ticks can infest large herds, ranchers are encouraged to consider the process of tick propagation in the wild. Female fever ticks live on their hosts for the ticks' entire life cycle, only dropping off to lay up to 4,000 eggs on the ground, usually in a pasture used for grazing. These eggs will hatch into larvae, which will then attach to animals that walk by. Without a successful management and control effort, such as an aggressive eradication program, the process will repeat itself over and over again.

recommendations for state and local agencies for controlling tick populations. They include creating and continuing public health programs that test for and track diseases and the mosquitoes and ticks that spread them; training staff in how to prevent and control ticks such as trapping and studying

The CDC recommends that states begin programs to deal with the epidemic of tick illnesses. This includes studying outbreaks, lab testing, educating people, and more.

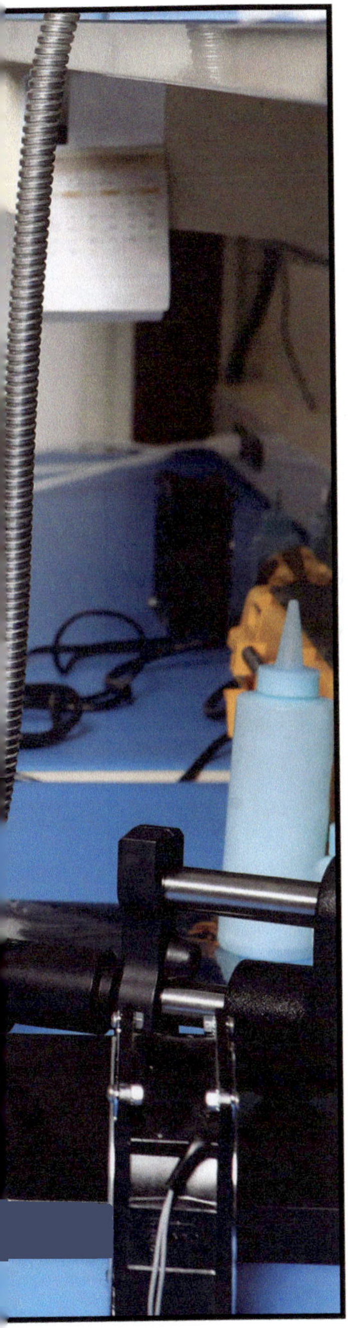

ticks, killing larvae and adults, and managing the environment to control ticks; and educating the public about preventing tick bites. The CDC also plans to increase funding to states for tick control, partnering with local agencies to detect and respond to tick illnesses, to improve laboratory tests for these diseases, and to help educate the public about what people should do to avoid ticks and what to do if they are bitten.

Ticks and the illnesses they spread are not going away. It will take both the efforts of scientists to study how to control and eradicate ticks and medical researchers to improve methods for diagnosing and treating these illnesses. It will also require people all over the world to learn about and follow procedures for controlling ticks on themselves, on their pets, and in their homes. It will take changes in behavior, especially for people who spend a great deal of time outdoors, as well as identifying and paying attention to the signs of ticks and tick bites. Perhaps in the future, children and adults will be routinely vaccinated to prevent these tick-borne illnesses, just as they are now vaccinated to prevent diseases like chicken pox, polio, and diphtheria. Until then, preparedness is still the best way for everyone to combat tick-borne illnesses and to lead healthy lives.

anaphylactic Having to do with a severe allergic response to something.

antibiotic A medicine that prevents the growth of or destroys microorganisms.

arachnid A type of insect with a segmented body and eight legs, such as spiders.

arthropod A type of animal with no spine, a hard outer skin, and a body divided into different parts.

bacteria Microscopic living organisms that can cause infection and illness.

cardiac Relating to the heart.

epidemic An outbreak of disease that spreads quickly and affects many people at the same time.

immunologist Someone who studies the structure and function of the immune system.

infestation The presence of an unusually large number of insects in a place, usually causing damage or disease.

larva The immature wingless stage of an insect after it hatches from an egg.

nymph An immature form of an insect that does not change very much as it grows.

orthopedic Relating to the branch of medicine dealing with correcting problems with bones and muscles.

paralysis The loss of the ability to move some or all of the body.

pathogen A bacterium, virus, or other microorganism that can cause disease.

projectile Something expelled with great force.

quarantine A place where animals or people who have been exposed to a contagious disease are kept.

rheumatoid Having to do with inflammation or pain in muscles or joints.

vector An organism, like an insect or tick, that transfers a disease or parasite from one human or animal to another.

virus A small infectious agent that replicates only inside the living cells of other organisms and can cause diseases.

American Lyme Disease Foundation, Inc.
PO Box 466
Lyme, CT 06371
(203) 785-3525
Website: https://www.aldf.com
Email: questions@aldf.com
The American Lyme Disease Foundation is dedicated to the prevention, diagnosis, and treatment of Lyme disease. It provides scientifically accurate information about Lyme disease to the public, as well as government agencies and the medical community.

Bay Area Lyme Foundation
884 Portola Road
Suite A7
Portola Valley, CA 94028
(650) 530-2439
Website: http://www.bayarealyme.org
Email: info@bayarealyme.org
Facebook: @BayAreaLymeFoundation
Twitter: @bayarealyme
The Bay Area Lyme Foundation focuses on the prevention of Lyme disease and also raises

money to fund better diagnostics, drugs, and treatments.

Canadian Lyme Disease Foundation (CanLyme)
Address: see website; offices vary by province
(250) 808-9978
Website: https://canlyme.com
Email: jimwilson@telus.net
Facebook: @CanLyme
CanLyme was created to provide advocacy and valid information about Lyme disease and other tick illnesses to both the general public and the medical community. Its website provides information about ticks, transmission, and living with Lyme disease.

Global Lyme Alliance
1290 East Main Street, 3rd Floor
Stamford, CT 06902
(203) 969-1333
Website: https://globallymealliance.org
Email: info@GLA.org
Facebook: @GlobalLymeAlliance
Twitter: @LymeAlliance

Global Lyme Alliance is a nonprofit organization that works to conquer Lyme disease and other tick-borne illnesses through research, education, and awareness. It funds research and creates education and awareness programs for doctors and the general public.

International Lyme and Associated Diseases Society (ILADS)
PO Box 341461
Bethesda, MD 20827-1461
(301) 263-1080
Website: https://www.ilads.org
Email: contact@ilads.org
Facebook: @ilads.lyme
ILADS is a nonprofit international medical society that focuses on Lyme disease and associated diseases. It promotes research and education into Lyme and provides support to physicians and medical professionals in treating Lyme and associated diseases.

National Collaborating Centre for Infectious Diseases (NCCID)

Room L332A
Basic Medical Sciences Building
745 Bannatyne Avenue
Rady Faculty of Health Sciences, University of Manitoba
Winnipeg, Manitoba R3E 0W2
Canada
(204) 318-2591
Website: https://nccid.ca
Email: nccid@umanitoba.ca
Twitter: @CentreInfection

NCCID works to create connections between researchers and the public concerning infectious diseases. It creates and operates networks and partnerships to help people with questions find answers and to support policymakers who act concerning infectious diseases.

World Health Organization (WHO)
Avenue Appia 20
1202 Geneva
+41-22-7912111
Website: http://www.who.int
Facebook and Twitter: @who

The WHO, part of the United Nations, is an organization that works around the world to promote good health practices, research into health topics, and universal health coverage. It also works to prevent and treat communicable diseases, including vector-borne diseases caused by ticks, mosquitoes, and fleas.

For Further Reading

Donnelly, Karen J. *Everything You Need to Know About Lyme Disease.* New York, NY: Rosen Publishing Group, 2000.

Faulk, Michelle. *The Case of the Infected Tick: Annie Biotica Solves Circulatory System Disease Crimes.* New York, NY: Enslow Publishers, 2013.

Friedlander, Mark P. *Outbreak: Disease Detectives at Work.* Minneapolis, MN: Twenty-First Century Books, 2009.

Hamilton, Robert M. *Ticks (Freaky Freeloaders: Bugs That Feed on People).* New York, NY: PowerKids Press, 2015.

Honders, Christine. *Bloodsucking Fleas and Ticks.* New York, NY: Gareth Stevens Publishing, 2016.

Kelly, Shannon. *Lyme Disease.* Detroit, MI: Lucent Books, 2011.

Kravetz, Jonathan. *Ticks.* New York, NY: PowerKids Press, 2006.

Lampke, Raymond. *Lyme Disease: When Ticks Make You Sick.* Detroit, MI: Greenhaven Press, 2018.

Merrick, Patrick. *Ticks.* Chanhassen, MN: Child's World, 2007.

Squire, Ann. *Lyme Disease.* New York, NY: Children's Press, 2017.

Bibliography

American Museum of Natural History. "99-Million-Year-Old Amber Contains First Evidence That Ticks Fed on Dinosaurs." December 12, 2017. https://www.amnh.org/explore/news-blogs/research-posts/99-million-year-old-amber-contains-first-evidence-that-ticks-fed-on-dinosaurs.

Bay Area Lyme Foundation. "History of Lyme Disease." https://www.bayarealyme.org/about-lyme/history-lyme-disease.

Bay Area Lyme Foundation. "Louis's Story: In His Own Words." November 18, 2013. https://www.bayarealyme.org/blog/louis-story-in-his-own-words.

Berry, Kevin, Jude Bayham, Spencer R. Meyer, and Eli P. Fenichel. "The Allocation of Time and Risk of Lyme: A Case of Ecosystem Service Income and Substitution Effects." *Environmental and Resource Economics*, July 2018, Volume 70, Issue 3, pp. 631–650. https://link.springer.com/article/10.1007/s10640-017-0142-7.

Centers for Disease Control and Prevention. "Lyme and other tickborne diseases." April 12, 2018. https://www.cdc.gov/media/dpk/diseases-and-conditions/lyme-disease/index.html.

Centers for Disease Control and Prevention. "Vital Signs: Trends in Reported Vectorborne Disease Cases—United States and Territories, 2004–2016." May 4, 2018. https://www.cdc.gov/mmwr/volumes/67/wr/mm6717e1.htm?s_cid=mm6717e1_e.

Columbia University's Mailman School of Public Health. "First Multiplex Test for Tick-Borne Diseases: Promising to Revolutionize Diagnosis, a Single Blood Test Can Now Accurately Detect if Someone Is Infected with Lyme and/or One of Seven Other Tick-Borne Diseases." ScienceDaily, February 16, 2018. https://www.sciencedaily.com/releases/2018/02/180216110532.htm.

Dimeo-Ediger, Winona. "Lyme Disease: Inside America's Mysterious Epidemic." *Rolling Stone*, June 20, 2017. https://www.rollingstone.com/culture/culture-features/lyme-disease-inside-americas-mysterious-epidemic-202050.

Doucleff, Micaheleen, and Jane Greenhalgh. "Beyond Lyme: New Tick-Borne Diseases On the Rise in U.S." NPR, March 11, 2017. https://www.npr.org/sections/goatsandsoda/2017

/03/11/519518318/beyond-lyme-new-tick -bornee-diseases-on-the-rise-in-u-s.

Elbaum-Garfinkle, Shana. "Close to Home: A History of Yale and Lyme Disease." *Yale Journal of Biology and Medicine*, June 2011. https://www.ncbi.nlm.nih.gov/pmc/articles/PMC3117402.

Gelman, Lauren. "13 Secrets Ticks Won't Tell You to Avoid Getting Bitten." *Reader's Digest*, accessed September 24, 2018. https://www.rd.com/health/conditions/13-things-ticks-wont-tell-you.

Harmon, Amy. "Lyme Disease's Worst Enemy? It Might Be Foxes." *New York Times*, August 2, 2017. https://www.nytimes.com/2017/08/02/science/ticks-lyme-disease-foxes-martens.html.

Hawkes, Logan. "Fever Tick Fight Adds Expense and Worry for Texas Beef Producers." Southwest FarmPress, February 27, 2017. https://www.southwestfarmpress.com/livestock/fever-tick-fight-adds-expense-and-worry-texas-beef-producers.

Johns Hopkins Bloomberg School of Public Health. "Lyme Disease Costs Up to $1.3 Billion Per Year to Treat, Study Finds." February 5, 2015. https://www.jhsph.edu/news/news-releases/2015/lyme-disease-costs-more-than-one-billion-dollars-per-year-to-treat-study-finds.html.

Kwak, Mackenzie. "Forget Ebola, Sars and Zika: ticks are the next global health threat." *Guardian*, January 25, 2018. https://www.theguardian.com/science/blog/2018/jan/25/forget-ebola-sars-and-zika-ticks-are-the-next-global-health-threat.

Liotta, Jarret. "What Is Lyme Disease? New Findings Deepen the Mystery." *National Geographic*, March 1, 2014. https://news.nationalgeographic.com/news/2014/02/140228-lyme-disease-borrelia-burgdorferi-deer-tick-science.

Margulis, Lynn, and Betsy Palmer Eldridge. "What a Revelation Any Science Is!" American Society for Microbiology. *ASM News* 71, no. 2 (2005). http://www.antimicrobe.org/h04c.files/history/znw00205000065.pdf.

Nelson, C. A., S. Saha, K. J. Kugeler, M. J. Delorey, M. B. Shankar, A. Hinckley, P. S. Mead, et al. "Incidence of Clinician-Diagnosed Lyme Disease, United States, 2005–2010." *Emerging*

Infectious Diseases 21, no. 9 (2015): 1625–1631. https://dx.doi.org/10.3201/eid2109.150417, https://wwwnc.cdc.gov/eid/article/21/9/15-0417_article.

Ricks, Delthia. "Tick-Borne Diseases Reach Epidemic Levels on Long Island, Panel Says." *Newsday*, April 12, 2018. https://www.newsday.com/news/health/lone-star-tick-sbu-1.17989946.

Wells, Julia. "After Tularemia Death, Experts Stress Education." *Vineyard Gazette*, September 13, 2018. https://vineyardgazette.com/news/2018/09/13/wake-tularemia-death-experts-stress-education.

Index

V

Y

About the Author

Marcia Amidon Lusted has written many books and magazine articles for young readers. She is also an editor, a musician, and works in sustainable development. She lives in New Hampshire, where ticks are an increasingly big problem. You can learn more about her books at www.adventuresinnonfiction.com.

Photo Credits

Cover Robert Körner/Moment/Getty Images; p. 5 Steven Ellingson/Shutterstock.com; p. 6 Susan Kehoe/Shutterstock.com; p. 7 Halfpoint/Shutterstock.com; pp. 10–11 Robert Nickelsberg/Getty Images; p. 14 Peter Dazeley/The Image Bank/Getty Images; p. 16 AnastasiaKopa/Shutterstock.com; p. 19 Dimitrios Kambouris/Getty Images; pp. 22–23 Dmytro Zinkevych/Shutterstock.com; pp. 30–31 De Agostini/R. Valterza/De Agostini Picture Library/Getty Images; p. 33 Crystal Eye Studio/Shutterstock.com; p. 37 Jrleyland/iStock/Getty Images; p. 41 Michael Sean O'Leary/Shutterstock.com; p. 42 © Paul A. Souders/Corbis/VCG/Getty Images; p. 48 BGSmith/Shutterstock.com; p. 49 Wellcome Collection, CC BY 4.0; p. 51 Napat/Shutterstock.com; p. 54 Katherine Welles/Shutterstock.com; p. 59 Szasz-Fabian Jozsef/Shutterstock.com; p. 64 Maridav/Shutterstock.com; p. 67 Runa Kazakova/Shutterstock.com; p. 72 Rocketclips, Inc./Shutterstock.com; p. 76 Davizro Photography/Shutterstock.com; p. 80 Michael Ventura/Alamy Stock Photo; pp. 86–87 Leonid Eremeychuk/iStock/Getty Images; p. 88 MelaniWright/Shutterstock.com; pp. 92–93 Stephen Coburn/Shutterstock.com.

Design and Layout: Nicole Russo-Duca; Editor: Elissa Petruzzi; Photo Researcher: Sherri Jackson